Suc[...] biscuit tin of life!

Andrew Townsend

ANDREW TOWNSEND

First published 2016 by Andrew Townsend
(Email: atfjpublishing@btinternet.com)

ISBN: 978-1539407805

Text and illustrations
copyright © Andrew Townsend 2016
Moral rights asserted

A CIP catalogue record for this book
is available from the British Library.

Printed by CreateSpace,
an Amazon.com company

AT
FJ

SOMETHING FUNNY ALONG THE WAY

For as long as I can remember, I have enjoyed relating funny stories, telling jokes and sharing anecdotes. My family and friends know I have always liked a good laugh. And my professional passion is for writing.
So in *Such is the biscuit tin of life* I am combining two of the things that give me the most pleasure.

This book came about after I made a New Year's resolution. I set myself the task of recording something funny every day; something that would naturally come my way, rather than having to be sought out. Now that has proved a little difficult because, to be honest, on some days there seems to be a dearth of humour about. However, the lack of funniness on one day is often offset by an outpouring of mirth and merriment on another.

The stories and comments in this book have come from far and wide, and I have aimed to provide smiles and chuckles for all members of the family.

I hope you enjoy reading *Such is the biscuit tin of life* as much as I have enjoyed writing it!

Andrew Townsend
2016

For all my friends and family
who have shared in the laughter
and fun.

JUST FOR STARTERS

A husband was a messy eater.
When his wife decided to knit him a jumper,
she was asked what colour it would be.
She replied, 'Gravy!'

A less-than-adventurous diner said,
'I won't eat anything... I can't spell!'

Joel Burger and Ashley King married in the USA.
Their wedding was backed by Burger King.
They had a whopper of a time at the reception!

When the 1066 Battle of Hastings was remembered
in England, there was a cookery contest...
the Battle of Tastings!

American actor Tom Hanks said he enjoyed shooting
films in fascinating locations – because afterwards it
made him a popular dinner party guest with his
mind so full of interesting facts!

A restaurant was run by
a man called Bland.
It served mouth-watering Bland meals!

A boss who favoured short meetings always held
them just before lunchtime... He found the
imminent break focused people's minds!

SWEET
BUT SOMETIMES
NUTTY

Fans at the annual Wimbledon tennis
championships could buy sunglasses in the shape
of... strawberries!

I learnt that a French couple
were officially stopped from naming their child
after the chocolate spread, Nutella.
They had to settle for Ella!

A boyfriend had a sweet way of proposing
– he gave his girlfriend
an edible engagement ring!

A bride wore an unusual wedding dress made with...
empty chocolate wrappers!

Question: What's a spaceman's favourite
chocolate bar?
Answer: Galaxy!
(Closely followed by Milky Way and Mars!)

Here's a piece of dieting and slimming humour that I
enjoyed: When I use the word exercise, I have to
wash my mouth out with chocolate!

I saw this sign in a shop selling confectionary:
Fudge is like most families,
sweet with a few nuts!

WHAT'S IN A NAME?

A man began to regret the name he had given his dog when he started calling out in the park. He sounded like he was barking, 'Rolf! Rolf! Rolf!'

American rock legend Bruce Springsteen, should he have ever wanted a chimney sweep, could have asked for the cleverly-named Bruce Sweepsclean! If he needed a cleaner, he could have contacted Spruce Springclean!

When a white van was given a nickname, it sparked speculation that perhaps the owner was a fan of the movie, The Sound of Music. The name of the van? Julie Vandrews! Another white van appeared to have been nicknamed after a Greek composer... Vangelis!

A spokesman for the Royal Society for the Protection of Birds (RSPB) in Great Britain was called... Mr Robins.

Shop owners have the chance to attract customers with clever names for their outlets. Here are three good examples: The Old Spokes Home (bicycle shop), Barber Blacksheep (hairdressers) and Tree Wise Men (ground maintenance).

A legal firm employed a woman named Mrs Coffin to draw up wills!

THE HAIR
ON MY CHINNY
CHIN CHIN

When there was a craze in the UK to grow
bushy beards, one group missed out...
the nation's firefighters.
They had to avoid growth on the chin
so they could safely wear breathing apparatus.
In an emergency, you would call
the clean-shaven fire brigade!

A member of the British Royal Family, Prince
Michael of Kent, who was known for his stylish
beard, was once quoted as saying, 'I have all sorts of
weird things living inside it!'

The best beard contest was a close-run thing. The
champion won by, yes, you've guessed it...
a whisker!

To keep your beard in order you may want
to visit the barber, Herr Kutz, or you could join the
line of customers expecting sizzling service from
Barber-Q!

A barber joked, 'I play with strimmers
for the shear fun of it!'

Joke: A row broke out at a moustache
and beard competition.
Contestants were bristling with rage!

A BRUSH WITH CELEBRITY

A group of friends, many years ago, were in a British pub for the evening, as was a man who had an uncanny resemblance to a pop star. The friends mercilessly teased the man for being a lookalike and the man happily went along with their ribbing. It was only later that the friends discovered the 'lookalike' had actually been singer Rod Stewart!

Jockey AP McCoy surprised his fans by announcing he was going to retire. On the evening after the announcement, a taxi driver asked his passenger if she had heard the news that everyone was talking about. She replied she had... 'I'm his wife!'

Keen fans of British actor Martin Clunes had the nickname of 'Clune-atics'!

'Celebrity' programmes on the television often attract people who aren't really celebrities in the true sense of the word. Viewers can be left wondering exactly who they are. Indeed, it has been commented of such people, 'They aren't even household names in their own households!'

A couple had a surprise when American singer Leann Rimes walked into their wedding reception by accident. However, from then on, they told everyone that the star had been a guest at their celebration!

PLANES, TRAINS AND AUTOMOBILES

Many years ago, a youngster was going to fly from the UK on a scheduled air flight to the USA. His grandmother – who had never flown – warned him... not to open the windows!

An airline passenger was hoping to make a two-hour flight from the UK to Granada in Spain. However, because of a mix-up, she ended up crossing the Atlantic Ocean and landing on the Caribbean island of... Grenada!

A commuter was travelling on the Tube in London when her train suddenly jolted. To stop herself from falling, she grabbed upwards for a rail but as she did so her arm went right up the inside of the shirt of the man standing next to her!

A motorist caused a stir by driving around in an open-top sports car with... a skeleton strapped in the passenger seat! Perhaps she thought a quick spin was a good way to blow away the cobwebs!

Crooks stole a car and drove it more than 200 miles across England. Police knew exactly what to look out for... because the vehicle was one of their own!

A bridegroom turned up to his wedding in a Batmobile... 'Holy matrimony, Batman!'

TROUBLES ON THE HIGHWAY

A weary van driver in the UK blinked his eyes open and saw a stationary car six feet in front of him. He slammed on his brakes, convinced he was going to smash into the parked vehicle – before realising he was already parked up himself...

A motorist was prosecuted for not driving with due care after he crashed into a sign on the outskirts of a village in rural England. The sign said:
PLEASE DRIVE
CAREFULLY.

A van driver hit a pigeon early one morning and feared he must have delivered a fatal blow. However, when he returned home in the evening, his wife heard a cooing noise and there, trapped behind a grille, was the unscathed bird!

A holidaymaker happily left his car in the care of a concierge service at an airport and flew off to the sun. However, he wasn't so happy on his return – dashcam footage showed his vehicle had been taken for a joyride!

A British motorist's first car was a model called a Fiat Strada. The driver said, after the car kept breaking down, it should have been called a Fiat Strander!

LET
THERE
BE LIGHT

Looking skywards, if you live in certain latitudes, you may be lucky enough to see the amazing Aurora Borealis. However, the glory of this natural spectacle has not registered with everybody. One individual thought the Northern Lights were in the UK seaside resort of Blackpool, famous for its illuminations!

A beach cleaner spotted a light bulb that had washed ashore. When he plugged it in, it still worked! How illuminating!

Fans of the Northern Lights thought they were in for a spectacular show when there was a spike in data picked up by special monitors. However, they were to be disappointed. The surge was caused by a lawnmower going too near the sensors!

A police switchboard in the UK lit up as countless members of the public suspected a glow in the sky was caused by alien activity. It's flare to say their concerns were unfounded...

A woman's plea was 'let there be night!' – after a powerful roadworks floodlight began shining straight into her bedroom!

Joke: A cleaner dusting chandeliers said it was light work!

VISITORS FROM ANOTHER PLANET?

People living by a British beach wondered
if they'd been visited by an Unidentified Flying
Object after a blurry image appeared in a
photograph. Their fears were put to rest when it was
revealed that the 'UFO' was actually...
a remote-control seagull!

Residents kept hearing a mystery humming noise in
a UK city. A sound expert offered two serious
scientific explanations – regarding mains frequency
hum and traffic noise resonating – but then added,
rather cheerily, 'Or it could just be aliens!'

In the days before astronomical events were
scientifically understood, a total eclipse of the Sun
would be a fearful event. Legend has it that people in
China thought the Sun was being eaten by a dragon
so they would bang their drums to frighten the
monster away! And it worked... every time!

Question: What's an alien's favourite
sweet treat?
Answer: Martianmallows!

When explorers from Europe arrived in the Arctic in
the 19th century, one set of Eskimos apparently
believed their ships had come from...
the Moon!

PITFALLS
AND
POTHOLES

One of the pitfalls of making historical television programmes is that modern-day technology can creep into view. A publicity photograph for the BBC's remake of the Poldark drama series, set in the 18th century, included a burglar alarm in the background!

Filming for another period drama was interrupted... when a low-flying military jet roared overhead!

In the present day, a mother was explaining to her children that computers had been around when she was a child. Her family had owned a computer with one game. The trouble was it was a snooker game and the computer screen was only black and white!

I enjoy snooker and would like to find out just a little more about it. I wonder if there is a book called The Potted History of Snooker? In the same vein, how about A Putted History of Golf or A Pitted History of Potholes?

One dark winter's night, while travelling home, I was following a van with a sticker which said something along the lines of: 'I'm not drunk, I'm avoiding the potholes!'

THE UPS
AND DOWNS
OF LIFE

In the harsh English winter of 1947, gangs of men were called out to dig down into the deep snow to create pathways. The work was arduous, having to be done with shovels, but there was an upside of sorts – on bright days the men got suntans!

Fans who 'crowd surf' at rock concerts sometimes lose a shoe. After the exhilaration of the 'surf', they face having to hop home! Oh, life's ups and downs!

Stress levels went up for a friend of mine in a department store. The woman's long dress became snagged on an escalator and the only way she could escape was by stabbing her clothing with a pen!

Question: Who keeps getting fired during his career but remains upbeat?
Answer: A human cannonball!

Ever had that sinking feeling..? You're not alone... Figures reveal 10 per cent of people are likely to drop a phone down the toilet during their lifetime...

My favourite holiday destinations are easy to reach – but hard to leave!

A tutor put down a student's work, saying, 'Plenty of dash, most of it slap'!

DON'T YOU JUST LOVE VALENTINE'S DAY?!

Valentine's Day can produce some revealing
comments. One man sent his love
'to the woman who puts up with me,
why, I don't know!'.

Another Valentine lover said:
'You annoy me more than I ever thought
possible but I want to spend
every irritating minute with you.'

I am fairly certain there was a spelling mistake in
this one but maybe the Valentine lover knew they'd
be together forever: 'Not only are you the love of my
life, but my sole mate.'

Somehow I think there was a little too much
domestic detail in this declaration of love on
Valentine's Day: 'Thank you for an incredible two-
and-a-half years of tiger onesies, playing tactical,
throwing clothes downstairs and being a buttsniff!'

Here's a sweet Valentine message:
'Love you lots, like Jelly Tots.'

A couple who had been married a long while
celebrated their wedding anniversary on Valentine's
Day, not by giving each other flowers or chocolates,
but with the rather mundane gift of... a door!

MEN AND WOMEN (1)

Putting up a touring caravan awning can be a challenging task. Caravanning couples can often end up bickering as the poles and canvas don't quite go together as expected. Indeed, such an awning has been described as 'divorce-in-a-bag'!

A woman who fell in love with a man called Mr Marriage was, I guess, soon looking forward to a wedding!

I saw this sign in a British fish and chip shop that was run by women and popular with male customers: If at first you don't succeed, try doing it the way your wife told you!

An amateur actor appearing in a stage play had a crush on one of the actresses – and kept forgetting his lines as he gazed at her!

A woman named Chris married a man called Mr Cross, thus becoming Chris Cross!

A couple showed how deep their love was... by marrying down a mine!

A bride had a castle theme for the wedding – perfect for her knight in shining armour!

MEN AND WOMEN (2)

This is a tale from the mining past of Cornwall in the south west of England. A miner had a falling out with his wife and she held a grudge against him. Deep underground the next day, he came to eat a pasty she had made for him. However, much to his dismay, he discovered it was full of broken crockery! His workmates, sitting beside him and eating proper pasties, thought it was hilarious.

A handicraft event aimed at women in an English city catered for their husbands with... a 'man creche'!

A husband had a surprise when he opened a present from his wife – and found a knitted jumper that had been 30 (yes, 30) years in the making!

A couple with the surnames of Makin and Shaw married. They were making sure they would be together!

Many British men treat their garden sheds as a haven. And a significant number use them as a secret hidey hole – with one of the items stowed away being... love letters from ex-girlfriends!

A bride started married life as she meant to go on – while on honeymoon she threw his husband's smelly socks out of their hotel bedroom window!

HUMOUR IS ALL PART OF THE BUSINESS

Economic downturns can prompt some dark humour. I smiled at this comment: 'Due to the economic conditions in the country, the light at the end of the tunnel has been switched off.'

After the 'credit crunch' in the early part of the 21st century, someone suggested public holidays in the UK, known as bank holidays, should be renamed failed financial institution holidays.

A man switched from being a banker to being a... baker – but he still had plenty of dough!

Two men of different European nationalities were in the midst of concluding a business deal. The British salesman closing the transaction said, 'Would you settle for 100,000 euros?' His Finnish customer looked interested but said nothing. 'How about 90,000 euros?' Still the customer said nothing. 'Okay, I'll settle for 85,000 euros!' The two men then shook on the sale. Years later, the pair met again. The salesman said, 'I remember you negotiated really hard over that deal.' 'Negotiated?' said the Finn. 'Not really. I was just trying to work out should I be saying "interested in or interested on" when you dropped the price. So I decided to stay silent and see how low you would go!'

FUN, OR OTHERWISE, AT THE SHOPS

In advance of November 5 in the UK, a motorcycle shop owner created a Bonfire Night Guy Fawkes using old rags and a pair of overalls from his workshop. To trick his colleague, he positioned the effigy on a motorcycle and left a note overnight saying: 'Look out for a guy who came in last night to look at a bike in the showroom. He said he would be back early this morning.' When his colleague opened the shop and turned on the light in the showroom he almost jumped out of his skin!

Here are some more clever names for shops:
Junk and Disorderly (secondhand shop),
Change of A Dress (dress shop),
The Merchant of Tennis (tennis suppliers),
Planet of the Grapes (wineseller),
Shutterly Fabulous (shutters),
Seams Perfect (dress alterations),
Suite Deal (furniture store),
Wreck-A-Mended (automotive repairer)
and Sell Fridges (they sell fridges).

A check-out girl grinned
as a customer wrote out a cheque...
in the name of Hazel Nutt!

A top florist was hailed as
the pick of the bunch!

DIETING
AND
SLIMMING

A health expert said the fact that a high proportion of the population was obese was a big problem. She was obviously correct in more than one way.

British actress Emma Thompson, when asked to share a favourite piece of wisdom, offered: 'Don't diet. Ever!'

A dieter was interested in the saying: 'I keep losing weight... but it keeps finding me!'

A slimmer aiming to lose weight with a keep-fit group exhibited a lack of optimism by calling it 'the keep-fat club'!

Dieters looking for a picnic spot may not consider Guzzle Down in the English county of Devon to be a suitable spot...

It has been observed that as people age, many feel more comfortable in their own skin – probably because it's a little looser!

Seen on sports clothing: 'Excuses don't burn calories!'

Question: How did the judge weigh himself?
Answer: With the scales of justice!

LAW
AND
ORDER

A police officer tweeted, 'Got to go to work now. Don't want to but people think I'm a responsible member of the community – and I don't want to blow my cover!'

A lawyer went by the name of... Sue Mee!

Joke: A container full of shirts and jumpers fell off a lorry and broke apart on the motorway. Police said there would be long delays for motorists because all three lanes were clothed!

A cheeky sticker on a young man's car said: 'Sorry, officer, I thought you wanted a race'!

A crook was a stranger to the truth. To try to establish the facts from him, the police had to read between the lies...

Police took a man to court over the theft of a bottle of perfume named 'Guilty'. He admitted he was.

Prison authorities in the UK were cracking down on inmates using mobile phones – and taking 'cellfies'!

And now for a tender tale. A dog put forward for service with the police was deemed to be unsuitable because it was... too gentle!

CREATURES ARE FEATURED

Chickens were filmed for a regional British news programme wearing hi-visibility vests. The firm that produced the vests said, 'None of the stars was camera-shy because they are now well eggsperienced in the hentertainment industry.'

A chicken farm was owned by a
Mr Hatch!

An album released by Universal Music was recorded especially for cats. Music For Cats aimed to leave the felines feelin' good!

A miniature donkey gave birth to a foal who weighed just 14kg and was about the size of a dog
– a dinky donkey!

Question: Which bird is always sounding off?
Answer: The cormo-rant!

A cat working at a British railway station
was given the title of
'senior pest controller'!

When a gorilla escaped from its enclosure
at London Zoo, it was commented
that things had gone a bit
King Kong...

MAN'S BEST FRIEND

A dad left his dog in the car as he went to the school gate to pick up his child. Every few steps he heard the car's horn sounding – his dog had worked out how to use the horn and seemed to be beeping at him to attract his attention!

A dog was content with being left at home while its owners went out to work for a few hours every day. The dog would take it easy, following its own routines. However, when the busy owners were at home on holiday, the animal sometimes found it difficult to adapt. As the owners began to realise this, they took pity – and decided to go out to give the dog some peace!

Joke: A dog was a deep thinker... he would often paws for thought!

Those who love dog walking may actually... find love. British television presenter Ben Fogle met his wife-to-be while in a park. Their dogs took a shine to one another... and so did they!

A dog walking business went by the name of... Central Bark!

A man chose his holiday destination on the basis that... his dog liked the beach there!

ALL
OF A
TWITTER!

A policeman put this humorous note
on Twitter: 'Atoms – can't trust them
– make up everything…'

In 2012, a British family reportedly
gave their baby the name,
Hashtag!

An ordinary Twitter user was asked
if he had any big names following him
on the social media website.
He replied along these lines,
'I have Henrietta Warmington-Carruthers
and Annabella Chisellingham-Fitzpaine
among my followers
– they are pretty big names!'

A showbiz reporter enjoyed a big name party in
Hollywood. Afterwards he said, 'I was the only
person there I hadn't heard of!'

Clever Hollywood actresses, taking a long-term view
of their careers, avoid having facelifts
– so they don't miss out on landing parts for
older women in movies!

A movie fan joked that while watching the film, Deja
Vu, he'd had the feeling he'd seen it before!

RELIGIOUSLY LOOKING FOR LAUGHS

Spare a thought for the men and women of the cloth who are expected to always conduct themselves in an exemplary fashion... One English bishop remained gracious even though he kept receiving the same gift. Parishioners in various districts revelled in presenting him with a certain bottle of drink thinking he would be delighted. However, in reality the novelty of receiving Bishops Finger had worn a little thin!

Sticking with bishops, one was heard to say that 'some people go to church religiously...'

In the Church of England, priests are sometimes given the title of canon. If things went wrong at a church overseen by such a priest, would the canon be fired..?

A church appealed for volunteers to help clean the premises. A notice was issued saying there would be a 'Bug Clean Up' the next day. An amendment was quickly sent out stating it was a 'Big Clean Up' but also saying there was no guarantee that bugs wouldn't be encountered during the effort!

Joke: A religious broadcaster was going to set up a new satellite television service. It would be a 'pray-to-view' channel!

HOWLERS
FOR
HOUSEHOLDS

A relative of mine was sprucing up his property.
While painting a bedroom wall with a roller, he took
a break for a cup of tea. When he returned, he found
his 15-month-old daughter using the roller to paint...
the carpet!

Another householder had a surprise when she
returned home to find scaffolding erected around
her property – by a firm which had got the wrong
address. It was enough to drive her up the pole!

A man went up onto a roof to fix a television aerial.
He accomplished this task but then his ladder
slipped and he was left clinging onto a chimney
shouting for help. Meanwhile, the owners of the
house were happily inside watching their restored
television service totally unaware of the man's
perilous plight...

A dog chewed through...
a neighbour's water pipe!
A howler's howler!

A young couple moving into their first home in the
town of Brixham, England, had a shock when they
went upstairs. There in bed was
a relative of the man who had sold the house
– and she was refusing to leave!

APRIL FOOLS' DAY

April Fools' Day is one of my favourite days of the year. I love all the harmless jokes and pranks. Take this one, for instance: a newspaper staff member was surprised when someone wanted to advertise a pot of stripey paint – until she realised what day it was!

A wife went to trick her husband early on April Fools' Day by dialling their home telephone and telling him he had a call. Unfortunately, she pressed the wrong speed-dial number on her mobile phone and ended up calling her mother-in-law who was still asleep in bed! Classic!

A news organisation ran an April Fools' Day story saying that a football (soccer, to Americans) team which played in a green kit was to paint its pitch orange, so that the players could be seen more clearly!

A public announcement was said to have been put out on April Fools' Day, on a railway line in London, apologising for 'any delays which were due to leaves on the line'. This excuse was improbable – because the route ran underground for its entire length!

MORE FROM
THE DAY
OF FOOLERY

Let's keep the April Fools' Day stories going for a little longer! The English football club, Arsenal, joined in the day of foolery one year by unveiling the world's first football designed particularly for... left-footed players!

Public relations companies often have a bit of fun for April Fools' Day. They make up spoof stories in the hope that media outlets will carry them to create amusement and to raise the profile of their clients. However, things went awry in one city. Members of a newspaper's staff failed to pick up that the PR story was a prank and eight days after April 1 ran a serious article saying that the outskirts of Norwich, England, could become home to a towering 50-metre sculpture... of a banjo.

As an April Fools' Day jape, a brewery chain said it was rolling out a pub menu specifically for dogs. Among the options was a... mixed growl!

Australian police mischievously announced on April Fools' Day that they would be mounting patrols in remote areas... using camels!

A British couple who won £53m in a lottery initially doubted their success... when they found out about it on April Fools' Day!

AND FINALLY...
(FOR SOME)

The kings and queens of ancient Egypt were buried
with items to help them in the afterlife.
Now it seems modern-day folk are
catching on to the idea. Undertakers report that
people have requested teabags, yoghurts
and bottles of drink. And, apparently, someone
asked to be buried with conkers
– that's bonkers!

People choose a wide range of songs and hymns for
their funerals these days. One person chose the
theme tune from the classic wartime film, The Great
Escape. Another, known as a joker by his friends,
had I Didn't Light The Fire at the crematorium!

In 2015, a newspaper reported the reburial of the
remains of the English king, Richard III, and stated
that 'ancestors' of men who had fought for the king
five centuries ago had visited for the occasion!
Spooky!

One of the most popular songs at funerals
in the UK in 2016 was Monty Python's
Always Look on the Bright Side of Life!

An elderly British man took the unusual step of
arranging and holding a wake in his memory
– while he was still alive!

RELATING TALES MAJESTICALLY!

An office worker in the UK decided to play a prank on a colleague by leaving a note, with a telephone number, which said: 'Ring Liz'. The number was for... Buckingham Palace, the London home of Queen Elizabeth II!

Queen Elizabeth II had a cushion which carried the wording: 'It's good to be the Queen'!

A foreign tourist visiting the town of Buckingham, 50 miles from London, enquired if it was possible to walk to Buckingham Palace or whether it was necessary to catch a bus...

Queen Elizabeth II's husband, Prince Philip, when he was well into his 90s, was about to perform the official opening of a new building. He had been undertaking such royal duties for many decades. Before he pulled the cord, he said, 'Pay attention, everyone, you are now going to see the world's most experienced plaque unveiler!'

Many househunters in the UK will pay a premium to live in streets with regal or titled names such as Royal, Palace, Lord and Bishop!

A family of ducks had a splendid house by the water – called Duckingham Palace!

OH, I DO LIKE TO BE BESIDE THE SEASIDE (MOST OF THE TIME)

Two children went to the English seaside
and had great fun digging in the sand,
especially because they kept finding 'treasure'.
As they dug, they came across more and more coins
until they had enough to buy their whole family
ice creams. They had a wonderful day...
Their dad was particularly good at throwing
the money into the sand
when they weren't looking!

One of the meanest pranks inflicted on children was
to tell them that ice cream vans only played music
when all the ice cream had run out...

A woman lived in a flat at the top of a cliff in the
English resort of Torquay. She had lovely views
across the beach and bay. But then a massive ferris
wheel ride was installed for tourists near the cliff –
with lovely views straight into her home...

A family was looking at a weather forecast on the
internet before their holiday to the seaside. One
member, who hadn't been paying too much
attention, glanced at the screen and said, 'Great! The
temperatures are going up every day!' Her
excitement was tempered when her relatives pointed
out that she was actually reading the dates of the
forecast – 25 to 31!

CLOTHES MAKETH
A MAN AND
A WOMAN

I was told that Victoria Beckham, before she became a Spice Girl, met David Beckham and established herself as an international fashion designer, used to ask to borrow clothes from a friend at college. I wonder if her friend is ever tempted to ask for the favour to be returned..?!

A UK charity shop running low on donated stock had a novel way of highlighting its problem – it positioned paper figleaves in appropriate places on unclothed window display mannequins with a message saying it was... down to the bare necessities.

I have a baseball cap which carries the slogan: 'I may grow old but I refuse to grow up!'

The crew of a ship acquired the rugby shirt of one of their colleagues without his knowledge and then proceeded to use it to clothe a dummy that was normally only seen when there were 'man overboard' exercises. The clothed dummy was photographed in various poses around the ship by the pranksters before the shirt was eventually returned to the man along with a set of humorous pictures!

A teenager wore a T-shirt that said:
'Please excuse my
embarrassing dad'!

MOBILE PHONE CALL-AMITIES!

It's strange how myths can catch on. One regarding mobile phones caused problems for the police in the UK. The story spread that if you called the emergency number, 999, and then quickly rang off, your phone's battery would get a boost. After numerous aborted 999 calls, exasperated police officers issued advice saying that the batteries on phones will only get more charge if they are... plugged into a power source.

A person wanting to use their mobile phone to thank someone couldn't get the predictive text message to say 'thanks'. Instead it was saying 'ugh'!

Be careful if you're reading your mobile phone while lying down – around one in six people have dropped their mobiles on their faces!

The obsession with social media can go too far... People armed with their smartphones have been known to choose a meal because it would look good in a picture – a feast for the eyes – on their social media feed... and then they haven't eaten the food because they didn't like it!

Joke: A pony was trying to make a call on a mobile phone but he could hardly make himself heard... because he was a little hoarse!

LOVE
AND
MARRIAGE

I came across this pearl of wisdom for men who have tied the knot... A husband's role is like any other job – it's easier if you like the boss.

There seems to be a mismatch in appreciation when it comes to marriages. Apparently, half of husbands in the UK think their wives are 'perfect' but less than a third of women think the same of their partners!

I had to chuckle at this humour... A wife said to her husband, 'I didn't say it was your fault – I said I was blaming you!'

A couple with the surname, Blanket, were said to have a warm and comfortable relationship!

A man going off to work told his wife that he would go around the world a thousand times to be with her again. And he did – because he, as an astronaut, worked on the International Space Station.

It has been claimed that nearly a third of viewers wish their favourite television character could be their partner in real life!

Joke: When asked the secret of their long marriage, Mr and Mrs Bond replied, 'Through thick and thin, we've just stuck together!'

SOMETHING TO SLEEP ON?

Nearly one in 10 couples in the UK
apparently argue over
who takes up the most space...
in bed!

Sneaky colleagues decided to quietly leave
a room after a fellow worker had
fallen asleep during a meeting.
The slumberer woke up hours later
– in the dark –
and the following day was presented with
a teddy bear to cuddle up to!

A guesthouse owner overbooked.
He had to give up his own bed
– and sleep in the garage!

A wife would nod off during the late news.
Her husband called it... the late snooze!

A new pop band that sang cover versions
decided to take the name...
The Duvets!

Birds in city centres
have been up all night singing...
because the neon lights have convinced them
that there is no end to the day!

FOOTBALL CRAZY, FOOTBALL MAD

As a fan, I often come across funny stories linked with football. If I were ever to go on the BBC television programme, Mastermind, my chosen subject would be the highpoints of following my local club. There have been so few, I should know all of the answers!

Football reporters can be prone to hyperbole. When one player was having a particularly good moment, passing the ball cleverly though an opponent's legs, the reporter declared, 'He's so good, he could even nutmeg a mermaid!'

During an English FA Cup match between Arsenal and Coventry City there was a partial floodlight failure. The Coventry fans, keen for the tie to continue, tried to be helpful by turning on the torches on their mobile phones!

Even though English football club Watford suffered some defeats, they still had Success on the pitch – a player called Isaac Success!

Football fans were celebrating on the terraces after their team won away at their closest rivals. However, the police told them to look miserable as they left the stadium so as not to further aggravate the home supporters!

MORE FOOTBALL FUN

Football manager Jose Mourinho said one of his star players, Samuel Eto'o, wasn't getting any younger and this caused much comment in the media. Soon afterwards, the player scored in a match and for his celebration he pretended to be an old man bent over with a bad back!

Another football manager was so upset by his team's performance that he wanted to join in with the fans – and boo!

A summariser said a footballer had had such a bad game that he would only give him a rating of one out of 10 – and that was for putting his shirt on the right way!

Police posted a message on social media urging motorists stuck in a traffic jam on a British motorway to stay in their cars and not take part in an ad hoc football match that some bored drivers had started. 'Please refrain from this activity,' said the police in a sober fashion. However, the first person to respond to the message asked rather cheekily, 'What's the score?!'

A football fan was despondent about the lack of speed in his team. He said, 'I've seen slow motion replays that have been faster!'

TIME FOR SOME SURPRISES

The world around us is full of surprises...
A woman living in England heard what she
believed to be the first cuckoo of the year.
The event was announced by a media outlet
but then doubts crept in about the report.
People commented that it was too early to hear
the migratory birds, but the woman remained
convinced she had heard the cuckoo.
However, a little later, while she was in her
garden, her neighbours called over to her.
They told her she had, indeed, heard a cuckoo –
but it was the sound of the clock in their
conservatory!

A commuter failed to turn his alarm clock
back an hour to UK time after holidaying
in France – and he only realised when he
arrived at the railway station where
he usually caught his train to work...
at 5.30am!

I was given a back-to-front alarm clock for my
birthday. Consequently, when everyone's clocks are
turned back an hour for daylight saving before the
winter, I have to put mine forward!

A receptionist at a hotel was asked, 'What time does
the 24-hour reception close?'

ALWAYS
BE
ALERT...

British Prime Ministers often face difficulties caused by their political opponents who close in on them whenever the opportunity arises. However, Prime Minister David Cameron was once troubled by another type of opportunist foe... A seagull took its chance and stole ham from Mr Cameron's sandwich while he was on holiday at the English seaside.

Another seagull took a large cookie from a child and then proceeded to swallow it whole. The sight astounded onlookers.

There are other hazards at the seaside... A loose dog took a large bite out of an unsuspecting tourist's Cornish pasty as she was sitting on a beach.

Meanwhile, a woman having a picnic in a park was flabbergasted when a dog roaming loose came up and licked her plate clean!

A homeowner in the British seaside town of St Ives had a sign which said: 'Beware of the dog – and I don't trust the cat either!'

In Bath, England, a sign said: 'Beware, two grumpy dogs and one grumpy man live here'!

DATES
AND
DATES

A newspaper in the UK caused confusion
when it reported that a person had passed away
on April 31.

A friend of mine was born on February 29.
When she turned 50, she'd actually only had
12 real birthdays.

A calendar published for 1988 in the UK could be
used again in... 2016. I guess if you hang on to
enough calendars from previous years, there must be
matches for each coming year.
Could save some money!

A woman said she was unlucky in love. And you
could see that she had a point. On one date, she went
to a party where the man she was with paired up
again with his ex-girlfriend!

If a potentially-romantic encounter doesn't go well, a
woman might be heard to say: 'That date was a total
waste of good make-up!'

A blacksmith hoping for a date was looking to
forge a new relationship...

Joke: On an awkward night out together,
two polar bears tried to break the ice...

PETS
AND
PONIES

Long ago, so the story goes, visitors to the pet department at the Harrods store in London were admiring a rather flamboyant new addition to the selection of animals on sale – until it was realised that the 'pet' was actually a white fur mislaid by a well-heeled shopper!

A British couple took on the care of two ponies. They liked the animals and looked after them but they wished they could change their names. However, the ponies would only respond to the names they were familiar with. So when the couple were greeting them they could be heard calling Tesco and Asda!

Another couple named their pet cats after two famous Americans. The animals were called Elvis Purrsley and Leonardo DiCatprio!

A pet dog was to take part in a school production of the musical, Annie. To familiarise the Labrador with pupils, it was allowed into classes – and, to make sure everyone knew the dog was meant to be there, it was given a special coat stating it was...
a member of the school staff!

A vet was said to have a number of... pet projects!

A glum dog was encouraged to be 'pawsitive'!

PICK
A
NAME

The owner of a pet cornsnake was inspired to name the creature after a cornflake manufacturer. The reptile became known as... Kelloggs!

A tortoise was given the name... Shelley! Contrarily, another was called Fluffy!

A couple wanted to give their soon-to-arrive baby the name of Faye. However, in the end they felt the name just wouldn't be fair on the child. A good decision, Mr and Mrs Moss...

A music festival had a spot where buskers could entertain the crowds. It was called the busk stop!

A group was reportedly upset by a village name in England, saying it was rude and should be covered up. But the name still remained proudly on show in Slackbottom!

There's a village in England that's usually quite quiet at night. It's called... Little Snoring!

Some drama groups become known by acronyms. One was called the Society of Harrowbarrow and Metherell Entertainers... SHAME!

I saw a van named... Harrison Ford Transit!

KEEP
A WATCH
OUT

Princess Diana asked English ballet dancer Wayne
Sleep if he wanted her to sit in the wings or at the
front when she was due to watch him perform.
The dancer advised the princess to sit at the front
because she'd get a better view.
Diana replied, asking whether he wanted the
audience to be looking at her or him.
Wayne quickly said, 'Sit in the wings!'

I was shocked to hear that some learner drivers in
the UK were trying to cheat their way to a licence.
They were hiring lookalikes to take their tests!

A plan to use a drone to film a couple on their
wedding day didn't go too well...
The flying device crashed right into the happy
(not-so-happy!) newly-weds.

If you wondered why colleagues at work were taking
so long in the restrooms, it could be that they were...
watching a television show on their smartphone!
People have admitted to streaming programmes they
just can't wait to see!

One enterprising garden shed owner
rather unusually decided to use washing machine
doors as windows. I hope he didn't get into
a spin when he installed them!

NOT ALL
IS WHAT
IT SEEMS

A number of Chitty Chitty Bang Bang cars were built for the classic film of the same name. One was deliberately crashed and was seen on screen in flames. However, that wasn't quite the end for the vehicle. An ardent fan of the movie later used some authentic parts from the wrecked car... to help create an eye-catching reconstruction!

Beach-goers in the UK must have had quite a shock when they came across... a skeleton! Fortunately, it turned out to be a museum model!

I smiled when I saw a novelty mug which carried the wording: 'I am the captain of this ship – and my wife has given me permission to say so'!

A British tourist returned home from a skiing trip with an injured shoulder after taking a tumble... in a restaurant!

A food scene was being filmed for the Downton Abbey television series. The trouble was some of the items of food were particularly pungent. To combat this, a member of the crew sprayed them with... disinfectant!

I once read that the secret of staying young... is to lie about your age!

HERE IS THE TRAVEL NEWS

One in seven car drivers in the UK admits to having been distracted by... attractive pedestrians!

A new one-way system was brought in for a town centre and it caused so many traffic queues that Station Road became known as Stationary Road!

It seems a train driver had that Friday feeling as he approached the end of his journey. In a public announcement, he said that the service would soon be terminating in London but he fancied carrying straight on with the passengers, going through the Channel Tunnel and spending the weekend together in Paris!

The spread of potholes on Britain's roads after several bad winters led to a new phrase becoming popular: 'We used to drive on the lefthand side of the road, now we drive on what's left of the road!'

A man in charge of laying out traffic cones on roads knew that some would be bashed up and squashed by passing vehicles and he also knew the financial cost this presented. He said the damage would be 'unwell-cone' news...

Sticker on the back of a car:
'I'm not lost, I'm exploring!'

THE POLITICAL LIFE

A politician standing for election was called Leslie.
To try to turn this to his advantage,
he used the slogan: 'Les is more!'

British Prime Minister Theresa May admitted she
really didn't like snakes, adding, 'That might lead
some to ask why I'm in politics!'

A British politician in the run-up to an election was
less than complimentary about some of his fellow
party members. He said that they thought optimism
was a type of eye disease...

Another politician, known for being prone to
slip-ups and sometimes saying the wrong thing, was
said to have the 'gift of the gaffe'!

British MP Jacob Rees-Mogg was quoted as saying
that raising an arm to hail a London taxi
was enough exercise for one day!

A driving instructor left time free after giving one
particular pupil lessons – the learner was a politican
and the instructor wanted to get his views across!

During a debate, a young politician jumped up to try
to speak, slipped on a speech paper – and went
flying! He certainly made an impact!

WAKING
OR
SLEEPING

My wife bought a mug which carried the wording:
'Sometimes I wake up grumpy,
sometimes I let him sleep!'

When a couple started living together, the woman
had to get used to the man's vivid and scary dreams.
While sleeping, he would imagine that the house was
falling down. Then, sleepwalking, he would lift up
the woman to 'rescue' her. Once she was dangling
out of a window before her partner woke up!

Another couple had similar problems. The husband,
having a nightmare in which he believed he was
being attacked, hit out at a bedside lamp!

A jet-lagged pupil went along to his school to pick
up his exam results. He discovered he had done well
and said he was going to celebrate... by sleeping for
the rest of the day!

Big moments in sports matches can play out for
many years in individuals' minds. Manchester
United star Ryan Giggs scored a celebrated goal
against Arsenal, finding the net after a dazzling run.
One of the players he went past was Martin Keown
who revealed years later that he couldn't forget the
moment. And he said he had even had a dream... in
which he had actually managed to tackle Giggs!

FUN AND TROUBLE WITH CARS

A car fitted with a towbar had a sign in the rear window which said: 'If you can see this, I've lost my caravan!'

The television comedy series, Father Ted, inspired the name of a car tyre firm – Farther Treads!

A day-tripper to the Dartmoor National Park in England left a car parked on a farm track, thus blocking access for the farmer. However, the farmer got his revenge... he used his tractor to plonk a large boulder behind the car, thus blocking the exit...

A man filled up his vehicle at a garage with the wrong fuel and had to have the tank pumped out. The firm that he had called to deal with the problem advised him to fill up the tank as soon as possible to get things back to normal. So the man immediately went over to a pump – and promptly filled it up... with the wrong fuel again! Hard to believe, but true. What a fuel fool?!

I've heard that some people who don't like their cars call them their 'loser cruisers'!

A British motorist caught speeding at more than 80mph blamed his dog. He said his pet had been sitting on the vehicle's accelerator...

45

NATIONAL AND LOCAL GOVERNMENT

A woman in a provincial city in the UK went shopping at a local supermarket and saw a man she recognised but couldn't quite put a name to. She smiled and said hello and then carried on shopping. It was only later when the media ran a report that she realised she had spoken to... British Prime Minister David Cameron who had popped into the shop on his way home from an official visit!

When Welsh singer Charlotte Church took part in an anti-Government march in the UK, the Observer newspaper said it was a case of 'Church versus state'.

Local government jargon can be baffling. And you begin to understand why when you hear stories like this one... An official complained that the draft of a new planning application form was full of gobbledegook and that people wouldn't understand it. His colleague replied, 'They are not people. They are applicants.'

Canadian MP Pat Martin explained he had to make a quick exit from a voting chamber because... his cheap underpants were making it uncomfortable for him to sit down!

Joke: A council created a regulation to keep town gardens tidy – it was known as Lawn and Order!

46

MORE FROM
THE POLITICAL
SPHERE

Wartime Prime Minister Winston Churchill paid tribute to the courageous Battle of Britain pilots by saying, 'Never has so much been owed by so many to so few.' Years later, some of the pilots joked that they thought he had been referring to their mess bills!

A pregnant woman was admitted to a maternity unit in the UK. She was asked if she was in labour to which she replied matter-of-factly, 'No, we have always been Conservatives.'

Blind British politician David Blunkett said that his guide dog was his best critic – when the animal started yawning he knew it was time to stop talking!

Joke: A member of the British House of Lords was repeatedly urged by his colleagues to get involved in a campaign for a burnt and mangled structure on a popular beach to be replaced. He was coming under... pier pressure!

Author Michael Dobbs was rewarded through the British honours system and became a Lord. This meant his wife could then use the title of Lady. Lord Dobbs of Wylie told how he informed his wife of her elevation when she was on her hands and knees with a scrubbing brush in their downstairs toilet!

THE RISE
OF
TECHNOLOGY

In a development that wasn't without irony, a
headteacher at a British infants school said that
some young children who used mobile phone
technology were lacking in certain social skills.
Smartphones were making them... less smart.

The advance of technology can leave people slightly
confused. I heard that someone once asked for the
location of the nearest App Store..!

One of my brothers said that his teenage daughter,
my niece, was surgically attached to her iPad and to
remove it could be life-threatening!

Around one in 10 Brits say they choose remote
holiday destinations... which are less likely to have
good mobile phone network coverage –
so they can avoid potential contact with their
workplace!

I've read that social media is having an influence on
the naming of some babies. In Egypt, a child was
reportedly named Facebook, while, in Israel, a little
one was apparently called Like after the Facebook
button!

Joke: A computer firm's false promise of 'free chips
with everything' was just a silly con!

PREPARED FOR THE UNEXPECTED?

A worried woman called the police after spotting a crocodile outside her house in the English city of Plymouth. The police, unfamiliar with dealing with such a dangerous reptile, rang a local zoo for advice. Then the brave officers set off to find out more about the fearsome creature – only to discover it was actually an inflatable toy!

Police in the French city of Vannes once found a drunken man apparently trying to give the 'kiss of life' to... an inflatable boat!

Joke: An ambitious balloon artist hoped his show wouldn't take off!

A British policeman said he thought that he had stumbled upon a significant haul of drugs when he checked over a boat in a remote location. However, it turned out the white powdery material he had discovered was actually... cheese!

A Boy Scout was selected to travel to a World Jamboree – but it wasn't quite as exciting as it could have been... because the event was only a 30-minute drive from his home!

If any man is going to be prepared for the unexpected, it must be a chap called Justin Case!

IT'S THE WAY I TELL 'EM OR THE WAY YOU HEAR 'EM

A woman misheard a British football fan describing himself as an 'attractive boy'. 'I thought he was showing off,' she remarked. What he actually said was that he was a 'Tractor Boy' – a supporter of Ipswich Town Football Club!

American singer and actress Bette Midler was in England. She was explaining how much she loved the country... 'And I love the language – I only wish I could speak it!'

A woman who disapproved of some aspects of the behaviour of her future son-in-law said that her daughter was going 'to have to put her foot down... with a firm hand!'

I read that British celebrity chef Jamie Oliver admitted he wasn't very confident when he asked a girl out on a first date. He said he was so nervous that he sounded like cartoon character Scooby Doo!

People sometimes get popular sayings slightly wrong. They have told of something being a 'damp squid' and of 'chickens coming home to roast'!

Joke: I knew a good singer.
She was called Carrie Oakey!

THINGS MAY GO PEAR-SHAPED

A naval dockyard apprentice was using a rope to carefully lower his mentor's toolbox over a dockside wall in preparation for working on a berthed vessel. However, calamitously, the handle on the box gave way and all the tools flew out into the thick, sticky mud below... The unfortunate apprentice spent the next few days trying to fish out the tools using magnets!

A couple jumping out of a wardrobe to spring a surprise on their unsuspecting victim had a surprise of their own... the wardrobe collapsed around them!

British television presenter Judi Spiers revealed that things threatened to go badly awry on her first morning on a programme when the autocue started running backwards!

Holidaymakers thought they had secured bargain flights from the UK to Sydney, Australia, but it turned out they were actually for... Sydney, Nova Scotia, in Canada!

A man said that he took a job as a cycle courier but had to give up – he had no sense of direction!

Question: Is a pear grower happy or sad when things go pear-shaped?

DESTRUCTION – ACCIDENTAL AND DELIBERATE

Gardening can go with a bang, a very big bang... A man's greenhouse was put up on the site of an old well. To start with everything went along very nicely with seedlings taking root in the warm conditions. Later, when the winter came, the gardener decided to protect his plants from frost by having a paraffin heater in the greenhouse. However, one night, naturally-occurring gas deep in the ground escaped upwards and found its way into the well. The greenhouse exploded.

During the Second World War, a Royal Navy man courageously volunteered to undertake the dangerous task of clearing a field of enemy mines after the D-Day landings in Northern France. He believed it would be a vital contribution to the Allied advance into mainland Europe in 1944. However, he said he later discovered the field was actually going to be used by the British Army... to play football!

A British insurance firm revealed that one garden slug created more trouble than could ever have been imagined. The small creature slivered into an electricity socket – and caused a power surge which broke a television set and a DVD player!

A gardener cleaning slippery steps called his brush a 'weapon of moss destruction'!

OFF TO
THE
SHOPS

A woman was queueing in a department store. The three in the queue in front of her were remarkably quiet and still. Aftering waiting for a while, the woman, who hadn't been looking up, rather embarrassingly realised they were... mannequins!

The town of St Ives, which I mentioned earlier in this book, has a district called Ayr. At the top of a steep hill, which leaves some out of breath, is a local shop. The outlet goes by the name of Ayr Supply Stores!

A coffee shop was named Brewed Awakening!

One is three UK shoppers said that they didn't visit shops on an empty stomach – because if they did, they would spend too much on food!

If you are having problems with your cycle and want to talk about them – and get them fixed – you may consider visiting a shop trading as Cycloanalysts!

A retailer selling produce including apples, pears and bananas had enjoyed a fruitful career!

Joke: When I went to buy a limbo dancing set, I tried to negotiate on the price. I asked the shopkeeper, 'How low can you go?'!

ON THE
RIGHT TRACK...
SOMETIMES

Train journeys in the UK have been halted by the 'wrong type of leaves' and even the 'wrong type of snow'. But a fallen tree wasn't going to stop a train getting through in a storm. The guard took the train's onboard axe and cleared the timber himself. Soon his passengers were on their way again – they clearly had the 'right type of guard'!

Question: 'What noise did the steam train with a cold make?
Answer: Aaah-choo, choo, choo!

Passengers on a train from London were left shocked when the service thundered right through their stop at Castle Cary in rural Somerset. It was later reported that the driver had simply...
forgotten to stop!

People have used some remarkable excuses for not turning up to work. For instance, an employee based in Glasgow, Scotland, contacted his firm to say: 'I missed the stop on my train this morning and can't get off now until London.' (London is more than 340 miles from Glasgow!)

A British politician said he hoped planned railway improvements wouldn't be...
derailed!

CREATURES GET INVOLVED...

The Romans left behind numerous artefacts when they retreated from Hadrian's Wall in what is now the north of England. Many have been discovered and preserved – and more antiquities have come to light thanks to... moles. Molehills have been found to contain pieces that have been hidden in the ground for more than 1,500 years.

I've been itching to pass on this piece of historical trivia... Ancient Egyptian servants apparently spread milk on themselves to attract fleas so that the pesky insects would leave their masters alone!

An aspiring pop duo recorded a song at home but admitted later that, if you listened carefully, you might just hear a dog snoring in the background!

Iron Age flints were brought to the surface at Land's End, England... by burrowing rabbits.

Members of a rescue team were called out to save a dog stuck in a hole in the English town of St Austell. They had a big surprise when they also found a cat... trapped underneath the dog!

A kindly firm decided to delay production in part of its premises when it discovered that a bird had chosen to nest and lay eggs in a piece of machinery!

ALL CREATURES GREAT AND SMALL

A report came in that a 'big cat' had been spotted in a city area known to be home to people relying on social security payments. One rather outspoken and cheeky wag suggested the area could be a location for 'benefits cheetahs...'

British Prime Minister Winston Churchill was a mighty orator but he once fell silent in the House of Commons as the attention of Members of Parliament was grabbed by... a mouse running across the floor of the chamber.

Concerns were raised over a 'neglected' donkey in Airdrie, Scotland – until it was realised it was a life-sized garden ornament!

A public plaque showing British choughs was repainted. However, it seems the birds were given yellow, rather than red, bills – making them look like Alpine choughs!

Question: Why was the cat sitting on the computer keyboard?
Answer: He was keeping an eye on the mouse!

Birdwatchers, who were reporting the sightings of various species, rather appropriately put up tweets on the internet!

BANANAS AND BANS

A zoo in Great Britain banned monkeys from eating... bananas. A spokesperson said that bananas cultivated for human consumption were too sweet and too soft for the primates.

Actor Hugh Laurie called for a ban on... bans. I'm not quite sure how that one would work, though...

A young boy I knew was sitting in the back seat of a car gazing out of the window. Noticing a crescent moon in the night sky for the first time, he exclaimed, 'Look, there's a banana!'

Question: Which pop group do monkeys like?
Answer: Bananarama!

One evening a couple in a campervan turned up at a quiet location in rural England. Another campervan was already there despite a sign which banned overnight parking. The couple asked the man in the parked vehicle about the sign. He replied, 'It is okay to park here overnight – I just carry that sign with me and put it up to discourage others from parking near me!'

One of the more unusual queries received at the Grand Central railway terminal in New York was, 'Can I eat a banana on the train?'!

FISHING
AND
FISHES

Question: Why did the angler always try to look his
smartest when at the lake?
Answer: He was fishing for compliments!

People have used preposterous excuses
to explain why they have submitted late tax returns.
One builder who missed the deadline pleaded his
case by stating...
his pet goldfish had died.

Golden oldie joke: Two goldfishes were in a tank.
One said to the other, 'Do you know how you drive
this thing?'

Letting agents found a home for three unusual
clients – goldfishes left behind by a tenant!

The most popular name for a pet goldfish
in Great Britain is... Goldie!

A man was found to be without a UK television
licence. He told inspectors he hadn't applied for one
because he only used the television...
to help his goldfish sleep at night!

Wife: 'I hardly ever see you, dear. Why don't you give
up fishing for a while?'
Husband: 'I can't, I'm hooked!'

ON
THE
PHONE

In a shocking example of someone dialling the emergency 999 number in the UK for an entirely inappropriate reason, a caller rang the police to inform them that her laptop computer was broken and she wanted a lift to the shops to buy a new one.

Unsolicited 'nuisance' telephone calls produce a lot of stress. One widower had a solution when he kept receiving calls for his late wife.
He told the callers that there was nothing he could do – his wife was in heaven… and he didn't have a telephone number for her!

There was embarrassment at a UK police 999 call handling centre when one of the workers there accidentally 'pocket dialled' the emergency number…

Just as a preacher was telling his congregation that God moves in mysterious ways, a mobile phone rang out loudly in the church. He paused and said, 'That's mine… I'm on call!'

Joke: A physicist was fretting over a discovery. A colleague called to ask him what was the matter?!

A school sent a text message to a father asking why his son wasn't in class. The dad sent back a picture of his child – on a foreign beach!

LIFE
CAN BE
CONFUSING

After my wife and I hosted a meal, we were given chocolates by our guests as a thank you gift. Nice! We then discovered... they were made for dogs!

When a young man living in the English countryside got married, his friends decided to spring a surprise – they tried to thatch his car!

American singer Dolly Parton told how she needed little sleep. Routinely, she would be up after just a few hours. However, when she was on holiday she would have a lie-in – and this caused great concern to her husband... who worried she had died in bed!

On departing from a job, a thoughtful teenager gave his employers a card to thank them – a card you would normally send after a bereavement... Whoops!

Leaving the house on a particularly stressful morning, I tried to open the front door by pressing my car remote control fob!

A UK man's first job was as a meal-time assistant at a school. Later he revealed that in the role, from time to time, he was referred to as... a dinnerlady!

'I Haven't Got A Clue About Anything Anymore'. A book by B. Wildered.

MEDICINE AND MEDICAL MATTERS

I chuckled at the bravado of a business which launched a range of products under the name of Man Flu – it claimed that women just didn't understand how bad men felt when they were unwell..!

It is estimated that more than a quarter of British workers have 'pulled a sickie' (taken unwarranted sick leave) because they were 'too tired to get up'!

Medication for children carried this warning on its label: 'Do not drive'.

Don't lie to radiographers – they can see right through you!

A caring medic was called... Dr Gentle.

A physiotherapist said that the data he was presenting 'limped' behind the latest available figures!

Joke: A woman being treated for a bad back by a chiropractor fell in love with him. Something just clicked between them!

A University of Manchester research project looking at the influence of the UK weather on aching joints was entitled 'Cloudy with a chance of pain'!

WATER
WAY TO
HAVE FUN

A group of British 'wild swimmers' who enjoyed swimming in rivers and the sea were due to compete in gruelling ice water swims in Poland. One said, 'It would be nice if some of us came back with some medals but I'm just hoping to come back really!'

I keep spotting the Loch Ness Monster... in flooding pictures on social media websites!

A couple celebrated their wedding by doing a bungee jump together above a river! They really took the plunge!

Young workers were tricked when they were each asked, as part of a 'competition', to balance a coin on their forehead and then try to drop it into a funnel secured in their trousers. While they looked upwards as the 'contest' started... their older, devious, colleagues poured water into the funnels!

An Australian had a plan for success when he swam across the English Channel... 'Keep swimming until you run out of water!'

A story appeared in an Italian newspaper during the Second World War claiming that the Loch Ness Monster had been killed by a direct hit from a German bomb. A myth about a myth...

DON'T LEAVE EVERYTHING TO CHANCE

People do the strangest of things in the hope of bringing themselves some luck. One woman taking her driving test in the UK wore the same T-shirt she had been wearing when she gave birth to her daughter seven years before!

You can't always leave things to chance. Consequently, you hear of sports stars who insure their limbs and models who have insurance for their looks. Well, to top it all, a tea firm took out insurance to cover its taster's tastebuds – for £1m!

Insurance companies in the UK deal with thousands, if not millions, of claims for vehicle damage each year. One of the more unusual accidents which resulted in a claim involved an agricultural vehicle... which fell into a badger sett!

Good safety practices... don't happen by accident!

British television presenter Eamonn Holmes selected this as a piece of wisdom worth sharing:
'The harder you work, the luckier you get!'

A 24-year-old woman didn't have much luck when taking the British driving test (perhaps she was wearing the wrong T-shirt?) but she eventually passed... at the 24th attempt!

SEALIFE
AND
ENJOY IT

A number of fish and chip shop owners have displayed a fine sense of fun. One called his shop, Phil's Yer Tum, another named an outlet, Frydays, while another went for Bizzy Plaice. Other names have included The Cod Father, Fishcotheque (did the customers dance with delight?), Chips Ahoy! in a coastal town and the Coronation Street soap opera's very own For Your Fries Only.

A baby was given the name, Ocean. Quite a nice name, many would agreed. However, did it really sit happily with the child's surname of... Haddock?!

A seafood week in the UK was o-fish-ially launched with a pun day!

An injured lobster amazed experts when it grew back some of its claws and legs in a short space of time at the National Lobster Hatchery in Cornwall, England. The clever creature was given the nickname, Clawdia!

A kayaker on the coast of England had a surprise one day... when he came across a badger swimming!

Question: Why did the fishfinger
lose the teatime race?
Answer: It let the tomato ketchup!

TUNE IN
FOR A
GIGGLE

A BBC radio presenter said,
'You can listen to this station
on FM, on AM, online and on...
your own at home!'

A weary traffic announcer on a local radio station in
the UK said that a particular set of roadworks, which
obviously affected his journeys, would be in place...
forever!

The BBC radio programme,
Woman's Hour,
was mistakenly said, on national television,
to have 3.5 million... viewers!

Question: What did they call the DJ who tumbled
over on the ice and injured his back?
Answer: A slipped disc jockey!

A regional radio station in England asked for song
requests on the theme of cooking.
A listener, inspired by his mother-in-law's efforts,
got in touch to suggest a track – David Bowie's
Ashes To Ashes!

Callers to a radio phone-in programme in the UK
were being told: 'If you've got something on your
mind, get if off your chest!'

NOT TO
BE SNIFFED
AT...

A sports pundit didn't come up smelling of roses when he referred to looking at something through 'rose-scented' spectacles!

A United States business selling bacon-scented underwear warned customers not to fall asleep while wearing the garments if they owned a large dog with razor-sharp teeth. Meanwhile, lion tamers, postmen and zookeepers were advised by J&D's Foods to steer clear of the unusual products!

In a twist on the above story, the business, based in Seattle, was also offering scented pillowcases – so customers could wake up to the smell of bacon!

Passengers said they were surprised by a downbeat announcement on a rail service in the UK. They recalled the announcer saying: 'May I remind you to take your rubbish with you. Despite the fact that you are in something that is metal, round, filthy and smells, this is a train and not a bin on wheels!'

A worker complained when she was referred to as a cleaner. She said that her official title was 'dust relocation technician'.

Joke: A father advised his daughter to work in a perfume factory, saying, 'You know it makes scents!'

MUSIC
TO MY
EARS

A musician was engaged to play in the background at
a function. He played tunes for around 45 minutes
and particularly impressed one of the guests who
had been sitting nearby. As the musician was
packing up, the man went over to him and said, 'That
was really great!' 'Thank you very much,' said the
musician. 'You can't beat the sound of the slide
trombone,' said the guest. After the initial praise,
this comment left the musician slightly cold...
because he was a saxophonist!

A nightspot set out to play pop music of a certain
variety as it aimed to be a 'cheesy listening' venue!

I spotted a white van nicknamed Van Morrison – it
was on the (Bright) Side of the Road!

The ringtone on a mobile phone
went wrong and began sounding like...
a pneumatic drill!

Question: What do you call a classical guitarist who
carries on performing despite being booed?
Answer: Plucky!

A television presenter once slipped up and
introduced pop singer Bryan Ferry
as Fryan Berry!

TALKING/SINGING AND NOT TALKING/SINGING

Telephone answering systems are taken for granted today. However, when answering machines were first introduced they caused some confusion. A mother rang her son only to be greeted by a recorded message. She didn't know what was going on and kept asking why her son wasn't talking to her!

I have another story from those early days of answering machines. When a secretary answered the phone with the name of the business she worked for, the caller wondered if her words were a recorded message!

British politician Clement Attlee once said, 'Democracy means government by discussion, but it is only effective if you can stop people talking.'

A pop singer who forgot the words to one of his old songs had a neat solution to the problem – he pretended it was all planned and said to his fans in the audience, 'You sing this part...'

The rise of technical wizardry has led to the emergence of 'silent homes'. A significant percentage of people living in the same house now communicate with each other via text, social media or email. Some even admit to using these methods so they don't have to talk face-to-face!

NUMBERPLATE LETTER COMBINATIONS

When I'm on a long journey by car I sometimes pass the time by spotting numberplate letter combinations that make words or form abbreviations. Some I think I would avoid if I were buying a car would be: VEX, LAX, SUE, PRY, BEG, OWE, BAD, LOO, FOE, OAF, YOB, MOB, MUD, DUD, DOH, CRY, SOB, HOG, TAT, WAR, SAD and UXB (unexploded bomb)!

I've come across some numberplate combinations that I quite fancy. These include: CAR, LOL (laughing out loud), JOY, FUN, ACE, TOP and FAB!

Here are more numberplate combinations – and my suggested uses. TEE or PAR – good for a golfer; REV – would suit a priest; BAA, EWE or RAM – a shepherd may like those; MOO – for a cattle farmer; HUG – would be appropriate for a friendly person; JIG – for a dancer; SAW – for a carpenter; WHY – for a philosopher; JET – for an airline pilot; and GIG or AMP – for a rock band.

I once saw the combination RED... on a blue car!

A car with lowered suspension had LOW.

And I had to smile when I saw a holidaymaker's car towing a caravan – incongruously it had SPY!

COPS
AND
CROOKS

Years ago, police were helping me after my car had suffered a puncture. 'Just checking that this is your car, sir,' said one of the officers. 'Yes, it is,' I said. 'We can't be too careful,' said the officer. 'Recently, we helped a driver to go on his way only to discover later that he was in a stolen car!'

Some people have names that don't suit their jobs. For instance, Mr Crook became a police constable.

There was a certain irony about the news that a burglar alarm installer... had had his equipment stolen.

Police officers had an unusual case in suburbia when they had to deal with a pig on the loose who was using people's flowerbeds... as a mud bath!

A mugger was caught because the person he targeted was having a picture taken at the precise moment of the attack – and the crook's face appeared in the photograph...

Two women put on disguises to rob a shop in an English town where they were regular customers. However, one was recognised after she neglected to put on any shoes – the shopkeeper knew she always went in barefoot!

SPACE, THE FINAL FRONTIER

An astronaut circling the world in the International Space Station would be asked by his spouse where he was. If he wasn't sure, he would invariably say, 'Probably above the Pacific!' The ocean is so vast, the space station spends a large part of its orbit above it, so he would be right fairly often!

When reports came through that astronauts were growing salad in space, people joked that they were cultivating rocket!

A British woman visited the USA in the 1960s and enjoyed watching a new sci-fi show on the television. When she returned home, she wrote to the BBC suggesting the corporation should broadcast the programme. However, the woman received a letter back saying that this would not be happening because the series would be of little interest to viewers. And the show? Star Trek, which went on to be a worldwide phenomenon!

Question: How many ears did the Star Trek character have?
Answer: Three – a left ear, a right ear and a final front-ear!

A Star Trek fan said that she knew her son was truly hers – because he had inherited her... sci-fi gene!

WORDS
ON
BIRDS

This story was told to me as a reportedly true one.
A boy went to a zoo where they ran an adopt an
animal scheme – people gave money and in return
were given a certificate and updates etc on the
creature. The boy seemed to enjoy his visit but on
the way home in the car he was rather fidgety.
Then, as soon as he got home, he rushed upstairs to
the bathroom. After he hadn't come out for quite a
while, his concerned parents knocked on the door.
The boy let them in and there
swimming in the bath
was a baby penguin he had 'adopted'!

A British farmer had a surprise...
when he discovered
a bird nesting in a pair of his overalls!

A duck waiting in a car outside a supermarket in a
provincial English town attracted attention – not
least because it was wearing a bow-tie!

An article on birdwatching
was written by a person called... Finch!

Question: Why was a player named Bird
selected for the football team?
Answer: He could fly down the wing, he was good in
the air and he glided past opponents!

HEY,
HEY,
BABY!

A baby in Scandinavia was said to have been given the middle name of Google. I searched on Google for the aforementioned Google and indeed he was there!

Two midwives were discussing some of the rather swift births they had come across. One told the story of how a baby in a hurry to arrive had ended up in the mother's tights. The other quipped, 'I do hope they were support tights!'

Stating your country of birth is a straightforward exercise for most people. However, for a small number it's not so easy – they arrived while their mothers were airborne. The birth certificate of one such person I knew said, 'Born in an aircraft...'

A couple had to get a passport for their child so they could fly from New Zealand to the UK to visit relatives. Achieving a suitable passport picture – mouth closed and eyes open – proved quite a challenge with... a two-week-old baby!

US politician Hillary Clinton would sing to her baby daughter, Chelsea, as she rocked her to sleep. Hillary believed singing to the little one would be good for her development. However, when Chelsea was about 18 months old she obviously felt otherwise. 'Mummy,' she said one night, 'no sing.'!

TALES
OUT OF
SCHOOLS

One of my sons was hoping to find someone to accompany him to his school prom. When he was in the school science lab, his friend pointed to a skeleton and said, 'You could go with her, she has no body to go with!'

A father dug up an object in his garden and wanted to know more about it. He gave the heavy, metal item to his schoolboy son who took it to show his teacher. Plonking the mystery piece down on a desk, the boy said, 'You're a history teacher, what do you know about this?' The teacher immediately recognised it... as a Second World War bomb – and the school had to be evacuated!

A school had a pair of English teachers called... Read and Reader!

British Olympian Kelly Holmes gave a talk aimed at inspiring school pupils to achieve their dreams – and she later admitted she was so pumped up by her own message that, when she got home, she went for a work-out in her gym... late at night!

A residential surfing school enrolled... boarders!

Pupils gained a good religious education from a teacher called... Mrs Godly!

DRAW A CURTAIN OVER PROCEEDINGS

A man said that the Scout Movement taught him to always be prepared. The lesson stemmed from when he was a youngster in Scotland. He was unprepared for the moment when the Scouts were allocated their kilts to be worn on special occasions. In fact, he was the last in the queue and ended up with a kilt that looked like a curtain on him!

Another man spotted a thread hanging from a curtain and decided it should be removed. Unfortunately, he employed his lighter for the purpose. The thread was, indeed, disposed off – along with the rest of the blazing curtain...

I guess an elderly person with a lot of worldly experience came up with this observation: 'You are never too old to learn... something stupid!'

A man said he liked it when lighter evenings came – because he didn't have to keep pulling the curtains over... to stop his neighbours spying on him!

Hypothetical query: Would you buy goods from a shop called It's Curtains For You?!

Wayward curtains had... gone off the rails!

OUT ON
THE HIGHWAY
AGAIN

The controller of a freeway gantry sign in the USA
became over-excited one winter's day.
The operator typed in a message for drivers
saying it had started to snow –
'and we are all going to die'!

Officials in the UK said that they opened a
long-awaited new main road, the South Devon
Highway, without any fanfare... in the middle of the
night – because they didn't want hundreds of
motorists queueing up to be among the first to drive
along the route!

A motorist misjudged a parking manoeuvre
and banged into refuse bins.
It was rubbish driving!

A bride wearing a resplendent white wedding dress
was seen heading for her marriage...
in the shovel bucket of a digger tractor!

Highways workers probably love some aspects of
their job and hate others. So I wondered what they
made of cleaning up a section of English motorway
after a spillage of... 20 tonnes of marmite?!

Slippery road ahead – after 24 tonnes of lard spilled
onto a motorway in Essex, England!

SMILING THROUGH ADVERSITY, HOPEFULLY...

Imagine a British pensioner's shock when he mistakenly received a tax bill for... £4.7m!

A bomb disposal squad in England was called to examine what was thought to be an unexploded grenade in a beach rockpool...
They found it was a fir cone!

Sign in a manager's office: One day we'll look back on this and laugh!

I've always enjoyed this combination of sayings:
'We'll know we're up against it...
when our backs are to the wall.'

A man in Stoke-on-Trent, England, was probably down-in-the-mouth...
after he accidentally threw his dentures into a fire!

A girl had a lovely laugh. People said it was infectious. Then she caught a cold and her laughter became contagious!

A man said his worst job had been a marketing role in which he had to call on people...
dressed as a baked bean!

MORE
FUN WITH
NAMES

Here are three more fun business names: Absolutely Barking (dog grooming), Curl Up And Dye (hair and beauty salon) and The King And Thai (restaurant).

A footballer in the English leagues lived up to his name when he blasted in a goal for Wigan Athletic. He was called... Max Power!

A floor coverings business operated under the name of Walter Wall Carpets.

Bluffing in business can catch you out. A new employee, who hadn't met all his colleagues, talked up one to outsiders, saying that Sam was 'a fine fellow'. It was then pointed out to him that Sam, in fact, was a woman!

A cafe at the seaside was called Coasta Coffee.

Customers were promised a good time at the Clock Inn!

Many names fall in and out of favour. In the early 19th century in Britain it is reckoned that around a quarter of all women were called Mary!

A young, new receptionist at a timber merchants yard was asked to put out a call for Douglas Pine!

YOU'VE GOT TO LAUGH AT WORK

A new employee was given what he was led to believe were two identical uniforms. The first fitted fine so he didn't feel the need to try on the other one. However, when he came to wear the second uniform, he wished he had checked it. He had to go to work in a shirt that looked like a tent on him!

Actors sometimes have to hang around for hours in between filming scenes for movies. This prompted British star Ian McShane to say, 'I get paid for waiting around – and I do the acting for free!'

A bus driver was spotted displaying this message on his vehicle: 'Don't follow me, I'm lost too!'

A worker using a very old computer was having trouble trying to create a Euro symbol. A colleague suggested that, perhaps, the machine had been manufactured before the symbol was created. The exasperated worker said, 'I think this machine was produced before hieroglyphics were invented!'

Industrial apprentices being subjected to pranks by older colleagues discovered one morning that... their toolbox lids had been welded up!

I knew of a man who designed rollercoasters. His career was full of big ups and downs...

A
RICH
TAPESTRY

A man who had turned 50 still had a fine head of
dark hair. A young girl innocently described him as
'the old man with young hair'!

British dads are apparently at their most grumpy at
the age of 40. The top three triggers are:
lights left on in empty rooms,
heavy traffic
and bad drivers!

Another grumble for dads is...
always being given socks
for Christmas!

A man was perturbed when he found out his bank
had closed his account and transferred the money to
a holding account – because he was believed
to have... died.

One dark night, a churchwarden went to conduct a
final check on a freshly-dug plot before a burial the
next day. However, he gave a passing motorist a real
fright. As the driver went by the cemetery, in his
headlights he made out the figure of the man
coming up from the grave!

Observation: A high-wire artist was always...
putting his life on the line!

GET
A
GRIP!

Many years ago, a person of some note in society was known for liking his drink a little too much. He was invited to give a speech at a function but had to cancel at the last minute. His representative explained, tongue-in-cheek, I suspect, that he'd been launching a ship that afternoon and his hand hadn't yet let go of the bottle...

A woman who was putting away her Christmas decorations after the festivities had a gripping experience she wouldn't forget – she got her finger trapped in a motorised novelty... and had to be freed by the fire brigade!

A man I knew had a very firm handshake – he liked to create a lasting impression...

On a rainy day, an announcer at a UK railway station was heard to say, 'Due to wet weather, services may be slippery.' (Should have been surfaces!)

A man lost his wallet when he went for a swim in the sea – however, according to a report, it was later found by a diver... in the claws of a lobster!

A team of climbers were set the demanding task of clearing a rock-face of an invasive plant... They were hoping to pull it off!

OF HORSES
AND
HOUNDS

Life was generally calm and peaceful on the remote
Isles of Scilly, around 30 miles off the English
mainland. However, the local police still had to
investigate a few incidents, including damage to
cars – which it was discovered was caused... by a
shortsighted horse!

I've heard there was a dog in London who, familiar
with a journey, would catch the Tube on his own!

A sign which warned dog owners not to let their pets
foul the pavement had a translation for dogs (though
I'm not sure they'd have understood it) – Grrrr...
bark, woof!

A dog owner had a surprise when taking the pet
along to church services – it started 'singing' during
the hymns!

A British couple were married at an unusual venue –
a horse rescue centre. You could say they were on
the bridlepath to happiness!

Question: What was the dog's favourite Hollywood
adventure movie?
Answer: Raiders of the Lost Bark!

A pub welcomed 'dogs with well-behaved owners'!

HAIRS
AND
HARES

A mum left her son in the care of her mother-in-law while she was away – but when she returned she was horrified to find her child had been allowed to have a trendy haircut she couldn't abide!

A middle-aged gent celebrating his birthday was given a 'hairbrush for bald men'. It consisted of just a handle and a buffing pad!

Historians recorded that
one of the fiercest Vikings
went by the name of...
Hairy Trousers!

A balding manager, who was having a very frustrating time at work, said, 'I'd be pulling my hair out – if I had more of it!'

The Beards, an Australian novelty band only writing and performing songs about beards, visited Europe with their Euro-Bout To Grow A Beard Tour!

Question: Who checks the hares' eyesight?
Answer: The hoptician!

Joke: Leverets keen to stay in shape went along to hare-robics classes!

OH, THE WEATHER OUTSIDE IS FRIGHTFUL!

I knew a man who moved away from the Scottish island of Orkney. He enjoyed his time there but said the climate was harsh. He told me, 'The locals joke they have nine months of winter – followed by three months of bad weather!'

An English non-league football club needed to defrost the edge of its pitch quickly ahead of a game one freezing night – so Bognor Regis Town drafted in a fleet of six cars to run their engines above the playing surface! The ploy proved worthwhile as the match went ahead and the team won!

The miserable weather in Britain in the winter often leads to people complaining. However, there is another regular winter grumble... about people who insist on wearing summer clothes – and then moan that they're cold!

Around a third of households in the UK admit to taking part in 'thermostat battles' in the winter. This quote neatly sums up the struggles over the level of heating: 'I like to be warm and my partner would rather save money – and wear a coat inside!'

Question: What happened when a
weather forecaster told a joke?
Answer: There were gales of laughter!

LIFE ON THE HOME FRONT

The process of making decisions about home decorating can become a power struggle among couples. A survey in the UK found that 90 per cent of women thought they were in charge while 65 per cent of men believed they called the shots!

A husband admitted he wasn't confident in the kitchen... He had low self-cuisine!

A family had a lot to live up to
– their surname was... Perfect!

A house for sale caught my eye – it was called Chuckle Cottage. Could be a fun place to live!

The old saying 'as safe as houses' took on a new twist when a developer in the UK proposed creating new homes... in a former prison. And it was promised that all the properties would be in good nick!

Joke: A customer asked if a certain model of vacuum cleaner would do a good job on a deep pile carpet. The salesman replied, 'My advice would be to suck it and see...'

Question: What did the cat do when his owner shut the house doors on him?
Answer: He got in a flap!

AS TIME GOES BY

Things don't always change too quickly in rural villages in Britain. Take, for instance, the village where one of my forefathers lived – Carnhell Green. In the centre of the community, a signpost for the local railway station was still in place... more than 50 years after it had closed!

A little boy from the county of Kent in the UK travelled hundreds of miles to go on holiday. During the summer vacation in Cornwall, he had his picture taken on the sandy beach in the village of Mousehole. Years later, he met and fell in love with a girl who happened to be from the village. When he showed the girl the photograph from his holiday, she was amazed to see herself in the picture, playing on the beach close behind him!

British Olympic cyclist Sir Chris Hoy obviously liked spending time on two wheels. After his top level cycling career finished, he mastered the skill of driving a Nissan stunt car... on only two of the four wheels!

A fellow elite sportsman, showjumper Nick Skelton, won a gold medal at the 2016 Rio Olympics – at the age of 58. He joked afterwards that, because of his age, fellow competitors in the Olympic village had mistaken him for an official!

OH TO
BE A
STUDENT?!

A new university student lacking knowledge of what one would assume were basic kitchen rules, ruined an electric kettle – when he tried to boil an egg in it!

Students couldn't quite believe that their tutor wore exactly the same clothes every day. His secret? Several sets of identical attire!

Plans were submitted for student flats above a public house... called The Skiving Scholar!

Joke: A sporty student complained, with mock anguish, that his trainer never gave him much praise. 'When I score in rugby,' he smiled, 'the coach just says "Nice try"!'

Catering students at a college in the UK celebrated the end of their course by putting plastic food wrap film to an unusual use – they completely enveloped... a car!

A young man at a university raised money for charity by going under the name of Sidney Harbour-Bridge!

Students concentrating hard in a hushed examinations room had an almighty fright... when a clock on the wall fell off and smashed to pieces!

MORE
THAN JUST
A NAME

A couple called Roberta and George had two
children who they named Robert and Georgina!

A man who had an extraneous 'a' in his first name
said that it had come about at the register office soon
after his birth. The story went that his father was
midway through spelling out the name when he was
asked by the registrar '"ph" or "v"?'. 'Aye?' he said,
'V.' And that led to the spelling of... Steaven's name!

A couple took on a dog named Leo. The only trouble
was that the husband was called Neil. So when the
wife called for either Neil or Leo, both would appear!

There was a highly successful motor dealership
salesman who went by the name of... Mr Carr!

A gent by the name of Mr Humble was described as
'a self-effacing' man...

There was a war historian with the name of...
Makepeace!

A grandmother said, 'I don't mind what you call me,
as long as you call me... to dinner!'

Felines could expect an excellent stay at the Great
Fir Cats Hotel!

ADVENTURES OF YOUTH

A young man at a festival was playing a guitar and singing songs into the early hours of the morning – much to the annoyance of fellow festival-goers trying to get some sleep in neighbouring tents. He wasn't the best of singers but one nearby camper recognised the strains of the Oasis anthem, Wonderwall. This camper, despite his agitation, had to smile when a friend of the aspiring musician was heard to say, 'That's great! Did you write it..?'!

Joke: A teenager discovering the joys of personal hygiene was confused. After wetting his hair in the bathroom, he picked up a new shampoo his mum had bought. The instructions said: 'For dry hair'!

A teenager was so late out of bed at the weekends and during school holidays that he earned the nickname of Midday!

A young man was due to meet up with a group of friends at one of their houses. His dad drove him to the house and was right outside – on the driveway with his headlights on – when a text message came through: 'Nobody else can come. Are you still coming?' With little hesitation, the youngster texted back: 'No.' And his dad, caught in a rather awkward situation, had to try to quietly slip the car out of the driveway without being noticed!

FOOD FOR THOUGHT

A top boss in the UK bemoaned the lack of dining etiquette shown by his staff when he met them... after one employee mistakenly ate his bread roll and, separately, another drank from his wine glass!

Here's some good advice I read: If you feel stressed, turn things around – and you'll get... desserts!

British actress Joanna Lumley let on how she survived kissing scenes... by chewing gum and sucking peppermints!

A producer of smoked salmon railed against a new regulation that said his firm's packaging should carry the words... 'Contains fish'!

A waitress had an order she wouldn't forget. The diner she was serving knocked into her – and a fish on the dish landed... on the customer's head!

A Biblical scholar said that he knew a little Greek – he served kebabs in the restaurant quarter!

The busy owners of an all-you-can-eat restaurant had a lot on their plate!

British actor Robert Bathurst said he enjoyed mustard and marmalade... together on toast!

HOSTING
AND
CATERING

Be careful who you invite around to your home... A third of women interviewed for a UK survey admitted to snooping through their hostesses' bathroom cabinets! They said they were interested in uncovering secrets, checking out beauty products and seeing how posh the toiletries were!

It has been said that a good hostess will always make her guests feel at home –
even when she wishes they were!

Question: What did the caterers bake for the police officers' party?
Answer: Cop-cakes!

A Swiss restaurant tried rather clumsily to translate its menu into English. Diners were informed that 'our wines leave you nothing to hope for'!

An arrested man had a cheek when he was being locked up for the night in a British police cell – he asked for 'eggs sunnyside up in the morning...'!

Plans for a coffee shop met with opposition. Discontentment was stirring...

A training college said it catered...
for chefs!

ALL PART
OF THE
JOURNEY

A bus company, hoping to attract more custom,
charged passengers only half the usual fare...
when it was raining!

A bakery wanted to cut the impact of its vehicles
on the environment – it announced it was 'slicing'
their emissions!

The hard shoulder beside a motorway is rightly
regarded as a very dangerous place to park – so I
was more than surprised when I heard
that someone had stopped there...
to have a picnic!

I've come across some unusual car names.
I particularly like the Nissan Micra Wave!
Then there is the Panda Mamy,
the Toyota Deliboy and
the Mitsubishi Lettuce (yes, Lettuce)!

Question: What do you call a guide leading
sightseeing trips on the Norwegian coast?
Answer: A Fjord Escort!

A farmer working out in the fields
in the morning would place
a tray of food on his tractor engine –
so it was nice and hot at lunchtime!

IN THE
SPORTING
ARENA

A USA competitor in the Rio 2106 Olympics
beat all her rivals to a gold medal.
Her name? Thrasher!

A cricket reporter suffered a mix-up moment when
instead of saying, 'The first test was drawn', he said,
'The first dress was torn'!

An athlete threw herself into the sport of...
discus!

A surfing contest underwent... a wave of change!

It has been stated, mistakenly, I believe,
that there is a lizard which likes to eat...
cricketers!

A young footballer was always up for the fight – his
name was Battle! And his teammate, Miller, would
help him grind out the results!

I heard that people were jumping at
the chance to work in a trampoline centre!

Ryan Giggs, when Manchester United assistant
manager, admitted that he stopped making
tactical notes during games...
because he kept missing the goals!

JUST
PICTURE
THIS!

Three educational establishments in the UK decided
it would be good to share lectures. It was agreed that
technology would be used to film a talk at one venue
and show it simultaneously at the other centres.
However, things didn't go according to plan with one
centre receiving only the sound and the other only
the pictures! The scheme was soon abandoned...

A relative of mine put her cup of tea on the floor as
she relaxed in the living room with her pet dog at her
feet. The homely scene was captured with some
video footage. On viewing the recording, my relative
was more than surprised to discover that the cheeky
dog had actually been drinking her tea!

A caretaker had to regularly jump on all the waste in
a large refuse container to compact it. His friends
jokingly threatened to film him in case he ever fell
over and the lid closed. If he had done, it would have
been a case of 'You've Bin Framed!'

A man in the UK rang the RSPCA for help when he
discovered a snake in his living room. The animal
charity asked the man what the snake was doing.
He apparently replied, 'It's watching television!'

A seagull was caught on a security camera... stealing
a £20 note from a cash box!

THE SECRET
OF GOOD COMEDY
IS TIME-ING

A tourist visiting the Scottish capital was reputed to have asked: 'What time does the 1pm gun salute go off at Edinburgh Castle?'!

A worker responsible for the public clocks in a European city knew how to wind up his employers. When he was leaving his job, in what he perceived to be less than satisfactory circumstances, he set all the clocks to the wrong time!

An artist wanted plenty of time for his next project... an installation involving hundreds of clocks.

A man boarded a boat thinking he was taking a 10-minute river ferry journey. To his dismay, he soon discovered he was on a vessel that had embarked on a six-hour coastal trip!

A couple turned up at short notice at a relative's house and said, 'We're staying with you for the rest of the year!' The relative laughed and happily let them in. The time was... 11pm on New Year's Eve!

A young sportsman had the surname Lock and the initial C.
I commented that his time would come!

Till the next time, goodbye!

ABOUT THE AUTHOR

Andrew Townsend is a British journalist and writer with an eye for the quirky and amusing. In addition to focusing on humour for all of the family, Andrew has written and illustrated the children's book, Belu The Whale, Lots Of Fun (available on Amazon and suitable for pre-school children).

Printed in Great Britain
by Amazon